THE BIG BOOK OF BELONGING

Can you find...

...the footprint hidden 15 times in
this book? Watch out for imposters...

The Big Book of Belonging is my way of celebrating the wondrous connections between us humans and the natural world.

From the air that we breathe, the food we eat, the adventures we seek, to the joy we experience, you will find a connection to nature in every single part of our being. And the more we can reconnect with nature, the more we can reconnect with ourselves.

I'd like to dedicate this book to all the children who like to climb trees, run barefoot, splash in puddles, search for bugs, sing with the birds, taste snowflakes and count the stars.

Because we all belong to nature and nature belongs to us all...

YUVAL ZOMMER

WHAT'S INSIDE?

Who is with us?	6
We are all unique	8
Home sweet home	10
Everyone is talking	12
Rainy days	14
Wonderful water	16
Family matters	18
Happy birthday	20
Growing up	22
Finding nature	24
Teamwork	26
Shedding	28
On the go	30
It's fun to forage	32
Seasons change	34

Sun seekers	36
The air around us	38
We are all connected	40
Across the world	42
Planet of poop	44
Brilliant bones	46
Seriously smart	48
Super senses	50
Give and take	52
Time for bed	54
Give nature a helping hand	56
Did you find...	58
Glossary	60
Index	62

WHO IS WITH US?

How many species do we share our planet with?

We don't know! Every day scientists are discovering new species in the oceans and rainforests, but there are millions that we know about already. These living things are divided into groups based on similar characteristics.

Mammals

Mammals are animals that have backbones and are often covered in fur or have hair, like us. Most mammals give birth to live young. Some, like whales, live in water.

Invertebrates

Invertebrates are animals that don't have a backbone. They include insects, spiders and crustaceans, such as crabs and lobsters.

Fish

Fish are found in rivers, lakes, streams, ponds and the oceans. They have gills to help them breathe underwater and most are covered in scales.

6

Birds

Birds are covered in feathers and lay eggs. Most birds can fly, but a few prefer to stay firmly on the ground or swim!

Plants

From tiny flowers to tall trees, plants come in all shapes and sizes. They are very important because they provide animals with habitats and food, and help to produce the air we breathe.

Amphibians

Amphibians, like frogs and newts, need a damp environment to survive. They like to live near ponds or wetlands.

Reptiles

Reptiles include crocodiles, snakes and lizards. They have dry, scaly skin and prefer to live in warm places like deserts and rainforests.

7

WE ARE ALL UNIQUE

What's so great about nature?

Every living thing is unique and special—nothing and no one is the same. From your fingerprints to the leaves on a tree, if you look closely you will see that each and every thing is different.

Fancy foliage

From a distance the leaves on a tree all look the same, but if you examine them closely you will see that each one has a pattern of tiny veins.

Standout stripes

Each zebra has its own pattern of stripes. This helps a baby zebra to identify its mother in a large herd.

One of a kind

No two tiger cowrie shells are the same. Each shell has a beautiful brown and bluish-gray spotted pattern.

No 'flake's the same

Snowflakes might look identical when
they fall from the sky, but if you look at
them under a microscope, you will see
that each one is completely different.

Spot the difference

It's not just a giraffe's long neck that
makes it stand out—each one has different
markings and spots on its coat.

HOME SWEET HOME

How do we make a home?

Every living thing needs a home—somewhere to feel safe, warm and protected. Just like humans, animals make their homes by building them from the materials they find in their habitats.

Small and snug

A harvest mouse likes to make its home high up in tall grass. It weaves a tiny, round nest just 3.9 in wide from blades of wheat and grass.

Shell swap

Hermit crabs use sea shells as mobile homes. As the crabs grow bigger, they need to upgrade, so they line up in order of size to swap shells.

Love nests

To attract a female, the male weaver bird carefully weaves a nest of grass. When the nest is ready, the female arrives to check it. If she doesn't like it, the male will have to start again.

Leaf lodging

The leaf-curling spider hides inside a dead leaf that it cleverly weaves into the center of its web. It takes a lot of practice to curl a dried leaf, so young spiders start off with fresh leaves that are more bendy.

EVERYONE IS TALKING

How do we all communicate?

Humans communicate using words. Around the world, over 7,000 different languages are spoken! Animals and plants have their own special languages too...

Show-off singer

The lyrebird from Australia can mimic other bird calls—it can also copy car alarms, chainsaws and human speech! Male birds attract females by performing all these noises and dancing as well.

Codes in color

Caribbean reef squid change color to communicate with each other. The messages vary from warnings of approaching predators to declarations of love.

Talk of the jungle

Tarsiers use a high-pitched call to keep in contact with each other in the noisy rainforest. They are protected from predators because the shrill sound can't be heard by other animals.

Protective plants

Fava beans can send chemical messages to each other through their roots. If a bean plant is attacked by aphids, it will warn its neighbors to prepare for an attack.

RAINY DAYS

Can we play outside in the rain?

When it's raining and we want to go outside, we can put on a raincoat or open an umbrella. But what do animals and plants do? Some hide from the rain or have found different ways to cope, while others are just made for wet weather.

Terrific tails

In light rain, an adult squirrel can bend its tail over its body to shield itself, using it like an umbrella.

Hide from the heat

A snail's body can dry out quickly, so it hides away in a cool spot when the sun shines. Snails are most active when it rains and at night, coming out to look for food.

Protective clothing

Butterflies have a special layer on their delicate wings to protect them from rain. The raindrop shatters into lots of tiny droplets when it touches the wing.

Perfect conditions

Mushrooms like to grow in damp, moist environments, so they wait for rain to fall before bursting out from just under the ground.

WONDERFUL WATER

Can anything live without water?

All living things—from a small seed to a giant blue whale—
need water to survive. Humans can't survive for more than
3 days without it! For the plants and animals that live in
very dry climates, finding water to drink can be tricky.

Clever cacti

Cacti have two types of root to quickly absorb water
from the ground. They store water in their leaves and
stems so their sharp spikes help to stop other thirsty
desert animals from eating their juicy leaves.

Sand bath

Instead of drinking water through its mouth, the
thorny devil lizard likes to bury its body in damp
sand after rainfall. It has special folds in its skin
that funnel water to the back of its mouth.

Thirst-quenching

During winter there isn't much fresh water in the cold Gobi Desert. Bactrian camels sometimes have to eat snow instead of drinking water!

Drink delivery

The sandgrouse has special feathers that soak up water, allowing the adults to carry it back to their chicks in the nest.

Brainy beetles

In the Namib Desert the fogstand beetle has a clever way of getting a drink. Tiny water droplets from the early morning fog collect on its wings and roll down into its mouth.

FAMILY MATTERS

What makes a family?

Human families are made up of different relatives, including aunts, uncles, cousins, grandparents and sometimes step-families too. Just like humans, many animals live with their families, staying with older relatives all their lives.

Eggs-tra care

White-fronted bee-eater birds live with their siblings, parents, grandparents, and sometimes even aunts and uncles. When one of the females lays eggs, the whole family works together to bring her food in the nest.

Female friendships

Generations of female elephants, including grandmothers, daughters, sisters and grandchildren, all live in the same herd. They have very close bonds and work together to protect and raise their young.

Special smells

Lions are very social cats. They nuzzle, lick and rub heads with each other to spread the family scent and strengthen bonds.

Caring canines

In an African wild dog pack every member is cared for. After a hunt the strongest members will return to their den and regurgitate food for pups and injured and elderly dogs to make sure everyone is fed.

HAPPY BIRTHDAY

Can you tell the age of a tree?

As we grow older our hair starts to turn gray and our skin begins to wrinkle. We mark our age with birthday celebrations. Animals and trees might not have birthday parties, but they still offer clues to help us work out their age.

Mighty Ming

The world's oldest animal was a 507-year-old clam named Ming. Scientists were able to work out its age by counting the rings on its shell.

Written in the scales

You can work out the age of a fish by counting the tiny growth rings on one of its scales—you may need a microscope to see them though!

Growing in circles

You can work out the age of a tree by counting the growth rings inside its trunk when it's cut down. One of the oldest trees in the world is a yew tree in Wales, thought to be over 4,000 years old.

Fossil feature

Rocks form in layers, with the oldest layer at the bottom and youngest at the top. Some rocks contain fossils of animals, like dinosaurs, which help scientists work out when the rock was formed.

GROWING UP

How do babies become adults?

All life on Earth starts small and gradually grows. Just like humans, as animals age they go through stages of growth, starting life as babies, then developing into children and finally adults.

Dragonfly

Dragonflies lay their eggs in water.

After a few weeks the eggs hatch into nymphs.

When the nymphs are fully grown they crawl out the water, shed their skin and emerge as young dragonflies.

Horse

A baby horse is called a foal. It can stand within a few minutes of being born.

At 4 years old, a horse becomes an adult. A female horse is called a mare and a male is a stallion.

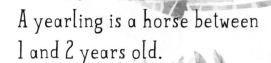

A yearling is a horse between 1 and 2 years old.

Frog

Frogs start life as eggs called frogspawn.

The eggs hatch into tadpoles and after 5 weeks they begin to grow legs.

After 2 years frogs reach their adult size.

After 14 weeks the tadpoles have become tiny froglets and are ready to leave the water.

Duck

A female will lay up to 12 eggs and incubates them for 28 days.

It takes 24 hours for the eggs to hatch.

After 50–60 days the ducklings can fly and are ready to be independent.

For the first few days the ducklings stay close to their mother, who keeps them warm under her wings at night.

FINDING NATURE

Why should we spend time outdoors?

Being outdoors is fun, there's no doubt about it, but did you know that it is good for you too? Spending time surrounded by nature* makes you healthier, happier and even smarter, so why not give it a try?

Noticing nature

Spending as little as 10 minutes looking at green spaces can make us feel more relaxed. That's because our minds focus on observing the nature around us, which stops us from overthinking or worrying!

Stop and smell the flowers

Fragrances like freshly cut grass or the scent of a pine forest can make you feel calmer and more relaxed. In Japan, people practice forest bathing—slowing down and appreciating the atmosphere of a forest.

Mood music

Some scientists believe that listening to bird song
can make us feel happier. These sounds boost
the hormones in our bodies that help us
to concentrate and focus better.

Let's dig in the dirt

Playing in the dirt can lift your spirits. When
we dig in soil, we stir up tiny bacteria (called microbes)
that we breath in. This makes our bodies produce more
serotonin, which makes us feel happy.

*Don't forget, no space is too small to make it green!
You can create a green space indoors by growing houseplants
or a balcony garden by potting plants in containers.

25

TEAMWORK

Why do we work together?

Sometimes we are unable to do things on our own, so we need help from our siblings, friends and classmates. When we work together we call this teamwork. Just like humans, different species of animals work together in the wild to help each other.

Someone smells good

The male orchid bee attracts females by releasing a scent that it collects from the orchid flower. The bee visits the flower, pollinating it in the process.

Open wide

The crocodile opens its mouth to let the Egyptian plover pick out bits of food that are stuck in its teeth. The crocodile gets its mouth cleaned and the plover gets a tasty meal.

A prickly pairing

Ants live inside the thorns of the acacia tree, feeding off the sap it produces. In return for the tasty meal, the ants protect the tree from any grazing animals that try to nibble on its branches.

Safe haven

Clownfish live safely within the stinging tentacles of the anemone. The clownfish are protected from predators and the sea anemone gets better water circulation because the fish fan their fins while swimming around.

SHEDDING

Why does our hair fall out?

Sometimes, when you brush your hair, a few strands will fall out. This is because we shed older hairs to make way for new growth in the summer and winter. Animals shed their fur, feathers and even skin to keep in top condition and adapt to the changing seasons.

Autumn changes

In the autumn, trees begin to lose their leaves. This helps the tree save water and energy for the harsher, winter months.

Keeping cool

In the warmer summer months dogs like huskies shed their thick winter undercoat to make way for a lighter, cooler summer coat.

Skin tight!

While a corn snake's body keeps on growing, its top layer of skin doesn't get any bigger. It sheds this old, outer layer to reveal new skin underneath.

Flight-worthy feathers

Canada geese fly long distances so they need to have very strong flight feathers. They will molt all these feathers at once, so for a short time they can't fly.

Attractive antlers

Male fallow deer use their impressive antlers to attract females and fight off other males, so it's important their antlers are very healthy. That's why they shed and regrow them every year!

ON THE GO

Are we there yet?

Humans travel all around the world to make new homes in safer places, to go on vacation, and to visit friends and family living in other countries. Many animals go on journeys every year in search of better food and places to raise their young, or to enjoy warmer weather.

Greener pastures

Herds of up to 100,000 caribou migrate each summer to fertile grazing grounds, where they have their calves. As snow starts to fall they return to more sheltered grounds and live off lichens for the winter.

Long-distance swimmers

Humpback whales have one of the longest migratory journeys of any mammal, traveling around 3,100 miles on average.

Mighty monarchs

The monarch butterfly migrates all the way from Canada to Mexico. Each butterfly knows instinctively which way to go from the moment it hatches from its chrysalis.

From top to bottom

Every year, the Arctic tern flies all the way from its breeding grounds in the Arctic to Antarctica—the opposite side of the world.

IT'S FUN TO FORAGE

Can we find food in the wild?

In the wild, animals find food for themselves by foraging. They will search for food resources that grow or live in the same habitats as them. Although we can grow some of our food, or go to a supermarket, humans also forage for things like wild berries, herbs and nuts.

Pantry preparations

The woodland jumping mouse has a special food chamber in its burrow for storing food foraged in the summer. It will collect seeds, roots, berries and nuts to snack on later.

Super stores

Chipmunks collect nuts and berries throughout the forest. They use their cheek pouches to carry anything they don't eat back to their burrows to save for later.

Prey perch

The great horned owl scouts for prey from the branches of the forest trees. It will catch rabbits, mice and hares, and likes to make its nest in beech, cottonwood and juniper trees.

A not so picky eater

The coyote will eat almost anything. It will catch rabbits, frogs, insects and sometimes even snakes, but will also eat fruits and grasses.

SEASONS CHANGE

Why does summer have to end?

The Earth is constantly spinning around the sun. When the Earth spins closer to the sun, the weather is warmer. Summer ends when the Earth is further away. If the seasons didn't change, it would mean the Earth had stopped spinning!

Spring into life

Spring is a time for growth and new life. Plants burst into life and turn toward the sun and children grow the most in the spring months!

Wrap up in winter

As the weather turns cold, we wear extra layers of clothing to keep warm and animals grow thicker fur. The days become shorter and some animals hibernate.

Bask in the summer sun

Water is in demand in the hot summer months. Baby birds start searching for food on their own, and fragrant summer flowers like jasmine and honeysuckle attract moths at night.

Play in the autumn leaves

In the autumn, leaves change from green to gold and orange and start to fall from the trees. Berries ripen and mushrooms burst from the damp ground.

SUN SEEKERS

Why do we love sunshine?

Almost everything on our planet needs sunshine. Spending time in the sun helps our bodies to stay strong and healthy. Plants need sunshine too. They use it to produce sugars that give them energy to grow green and tall.

Searching for sun

Giant elephant ear plants have leaves that are up to 5.9 ft long so that they can capture as much sunlight as possible down on the shady jungle floor.

Snoozing in sunshine

Cats will often be found snoozing in a sunny spot. This is because their body temperature drops when they sleep, so the sun keeps them warm.

Feather care

Blackbirds like to stretch out their wings and sunbathe. The sunshine helps to spread the preen oil that keeps their feathers waterproof and flexible, and drives out any pesky parasites.

Body warmers

Cold-blooded reptiles like lizards can't generate their own body heat so they need to bask in the sun to keep their energy levels up.

Keeping track

Daisies close their petals at night and open them in the morning light. The flowers will follow the sun as it moves across the sky throughout the day.

THE AIR AROUND US

How does the air stay clean?

We breathe in oxygen and breathe out carbon dioxide. Too much carbon dioxide is contributing to global warming, but luckily plants absorb carbon dioxide from the air and release oxygen instead. So the more we look after plants and trees, the more carbon dioxide they can help absorb from the atmosphere.

The lungs of the Earth

Each and every tree in the Amazon rainforest helps to make lots of oxygen and absorb carbon dioxide. Wild fires are happening in the Amazon more and more, though, so we need to protect it to help prevent climate change.

Awesome oceans

The oceans absorb large amounts of the carbon dioxide produced on Earth. It's not just absorbed in the water though. Algae, coral and seaweed can also absorb it and so can plankton (and the whales that eat them) too!

Fabulous forests

Kelp forests are very important to the planet because they absorb so much carbon dioxide. The giant underwater forests along the coast of California are some of the biggest in the world.

Sensational seagrass

Seagrass grows in shallow areas so that it can use the sun's energy to grow underwater! 11 square feet of seagrass can make over 2.5 gallons of oxygen every day.

WE ARE ALL CONNECTED

What is an ecosystem?

An ecosystem is a community of living things that share an environment together. All living things in an ecosystem depend on each other, which is why humans have to be careful not to damage these environments. It doesn't matter where in the world you live, you are part of an ecosystem, maybe more than one. Ecosystems can be big like a whole rainforest or small like a pond.

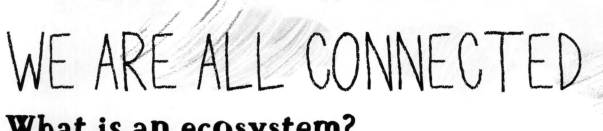

Damselflies like to feed in the grasses that grow near this pond.

Old logs and stones provide shelter for newts and toads in the late summer months.

Tadpoles need shallow, sunny areas during the daytime and deeper water where they can hide at night.

For moorhens, pond vegetation provides food as well as a safe place to sleep at night.

Dragonflies lay their eggs on plant stems or leaves close to the surface of the water.

Pond weed is a favorite food source for ducks and makes a great hiding place for frogs.

41

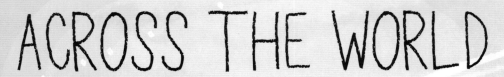

ACROSS THE WORLD

Is it cold for everyone in December?

Because the Earth rotates as it travels around the sun, the conditions we experience change depending on where in the world we live. If you live on the opposite side of the planet from your friend or relative the chances are the time of day, the weather and even the season might be different for each of you.

Summer months

In the Northern Hemisphere summer falls in June, July and August and winter is in December, January and February. In the Southern Hemisphere the seasons are the other way around. So if you live in Australia, Christmas is in the middle of summer!

Special shadows

Did you know that the direction of your shadow changes in different parts of the world? In the Northern Hemisphere your shadow will point north at noon and in the Southern Hemisphere, it will point south.

Swirling, whirling water

Large whirlpools in the Southern Hemisphere tend to spin clockwise, while whirlpools in the Northern Hemisphere spin counterclockwise. Some people think the same thing happens in bath tubs!

Spinning around

In the Southern Hemisphere storms like hurricanes or typhoons spin clockwise, but in the Northern Hemisphere they spin in the opposite direction.

PLANET OF POOP

What's the point of poop?

Almost every animal on the planet poops but what's the point of it? A lot of animal poop is actually very useful— it spreads seeds, which helps forests, farms and gardens to grow. For some animals it even makes a tasty treat...

Gardener's delight

Farmers and gardeners like to add horse or cow poop to the soil. The poop, called manure, adds nutrients to the earth, which produces stronger crops with more flowers, fruit and vegetables.

Great balls of...poop

When a dung beetle spots some elephant or rhino poop it will quickly shape it into a ball and roll it away. The beetles eat the poop and use it to lay their eggs in.

Treetop toilets

The Australian mistletoe bird likes to eat the berries produced by mistletoe. The bird's poop is full of the seeds, which are spread from tree to tree as it flies around.

Fishy friends

In the Pantanal wetlands in Brazil, plants drop their fruits during the wet season when the ground is flooded. The fish eat the fallen fruit and then spread the seeds in their poop wherever they swim.

BRILLIANT BONES

How do our bodies help us move?

Every single person has a skeleton made up of lots of different types of bones. These bones give your body shape and help you move. Skeletons can tell you a lot about an animal's abilities—we learned everything we know about dinosaurs from their bones!

Backward bats

At the end of each of a bat's arms it has 4 thin and extremely long fingers that act as the frame for its wings. A bat also has backward leg bones so that it can hang upside down by its feet when it sleeps.

Built for speed

A cheetah's skeleton is designed for speed. It has extra-long leg bones and a flexible spine, and can cover 22 ft with each stride.

As bendy as can be

The green tree python needs to be able to wrap itself tightly around tree branches or prey. A snake's spine is very long and it has hundreds of ribs that run almost the entire length of its body, making it strong and flexible.

Light as a feather

The peregrine falcon can fly at speeds of up to 200 miles per hour. It has hollow bones to keep its body light and help use as little energy as possible when flying.

SERIOUSLY SMART

Who is the smartest?

Every human has a brain. We use our brains for problem-solving, being creative and to learn. Just like us, animals can be very intelligent.

Squirrel sabotage

Squirrels hide food so that they have a supply throughout the winter. Sometimes they will pretend to bury food to trick any other animals that are watching.

Mammal in the mirror

Dolphins are one of the most intelligent animals and scientists have discovered that they can recognize their own reflection in a mirror.

Homemade armor

Some species of octopus have figured out that coconut shells can be used as a handy hiding place. They carry a coconut shell with them and use it as armor if they feel threatened.

Music makers

A male palm cockatoo uses twigs and seed
pods as musical instruments to impress
a potential mate. Each male has his own
musical rhythm as he beats his tools against
hollow trees like drums.

Farmer ants

Leafcutter ants carry leaves back to their mound,
where they chew them up and spit them back out.
This encourages a special fungus to grow. The ants
farm the fungus safely in their colony and harvest
it when they are hungry.

SUPER SENSES

Why do we have senses?

Our senses allow us to understand the world around us and are particularly good at keeping us out of danger. Some animals have far sharper senses than humans.

Tongue twister

Snakes don't have noses like humans. They have nostrils for breathing but smell by flicking their tongues to pick up scents in the air. This helps them detect danger (or prey) nearby.

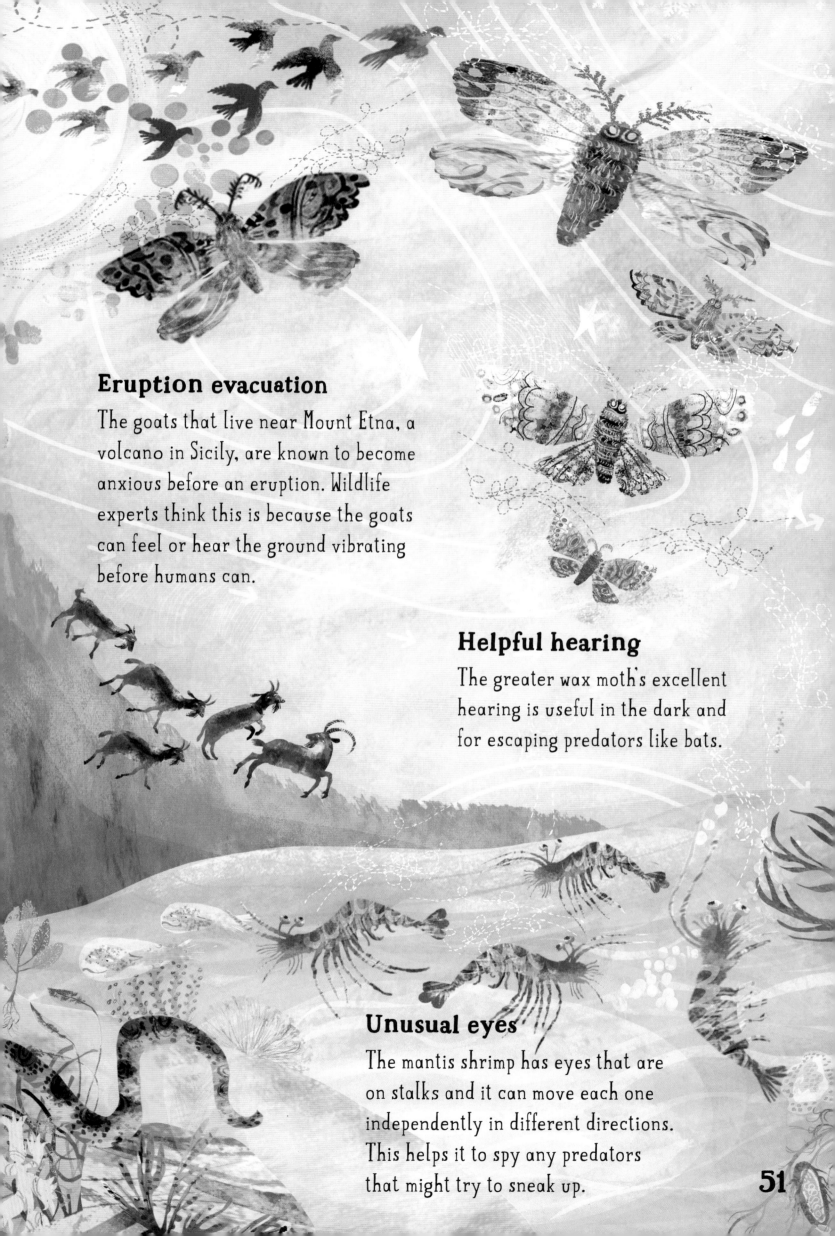

Eruption evacuation

The goats that live near Mount Etna, a volcano in Sicily, are known to become anxious before an eruption. Wildlife experts think this is because the goats can feel or hear the ground vibrating before humans can.

Helpful hearing

The greater wax moth's excellent hearing is useful in the dark and for escaping predators like bats.

Unusual eyes

The mantis shrimp has eyes that are on stalks and it can move each one independently in different directions. This helps it to spy any predators that might try to sneak up.

GIVE AND TAKE

What do we make things from?

Materials! A material is something that we use to make an object. Sometimes these materials come from nature like plants, animals or the ground, but other times they can be man-made. Whatever we make an item from, we always have to be careful about not using too much!

Wonderful wood

Did you know that the pencil and paper that you use for writing are made from trees? It is important that we recycle paper so that we don't have to cut down too many trees.

Cool clothing

Lots of the clothes we wear are made from materials like cotton or wool. Cotton comes from the seed fibers of a cotton plant and wool comes from animals like sheep or goats.

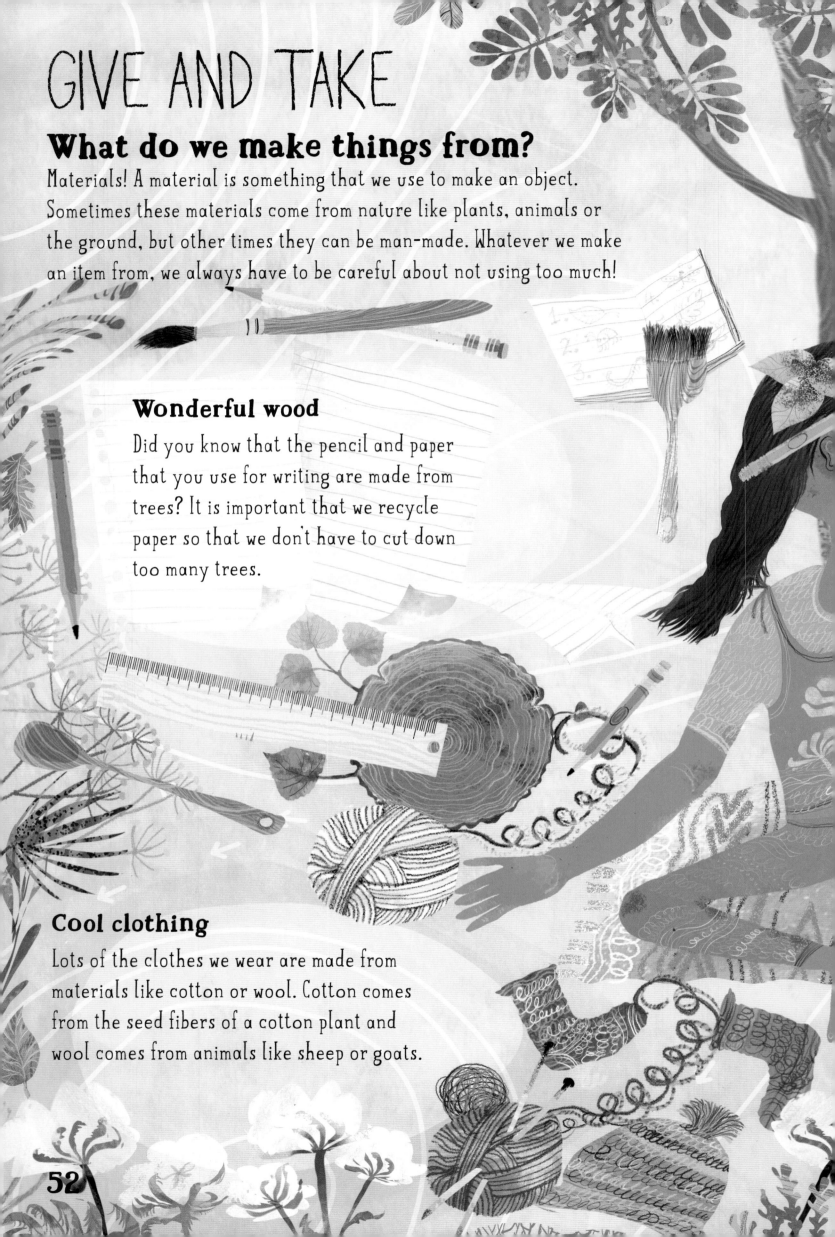

Made from mud

If you look around your home right now, you will probably spot something made of clay. Clay is a natural material found underground that goes very hard when it dries. It can be made into bricks and planters, or even a mug to drink hot chocolate from!

Problematic plastic

Sadly, a lot of the things we use, like water bottles and toothbrushes, are made from plastic. The problem with plastic is that it can't rot like paper or food so it stays on our planet. It's really important to try and reuse plastic items or, better yet, use alternatives like glass bottles or bamboo toothbrushes!

What to do with trash?

Throwing trash away in the wrong place can be harmful to animals and their habitats. That's why it's important to make sure we put trash in the trashcan. Plastic, metals, glass and even food can all be recycled, which means they can be used again and again!

TIME FOR BED

Do we have to go to sleep now?

Every creature needs to rest. Just like eating, sleep is essential for survival as it gives your body time to relax and get ready for the next day. We like to sleep in a soft bed, but some animals have very different ways of taking a nap.

Standing snooze

Cows lock their legs so that they can sleep while standing up. This makes it much easier for them to run away from predators at night.

Hold tight

Sea otters wrap themselves in seaweed and hold hands (or paws) when it is time for them to go to bed. This stops them from drifting apart while they are asleep.

Alarm calls

As the sun starts to set, kookaburras gather together in trees to roost for the night. When the sun rises, they all call out together, making quite a lot of noise.

Kip when it's cold

Butterflies rest from late afternoon because they can't fly when it gets cold at night. They hide under large leaves or branches and wait for it to warm up again in the morning.

GIVE NATURE A HELPING HAND

How can we help the nature around us?

Whether you've got a balcony, a garden or just a few flower pots, nature is all around you and needs your help. The best way to support nature and encourage wildlife is to make sure that animals have plenty of safe places to live and lots of food.

Save the weeds

Let areas of your garden grow wild. Weeds like dandelions and stinging nettles support all sorts of wildlife, providing food for bees, butterflies and other important pollinators.

Make a toad abode

Dig a hole about 12 in deep and fill it with logs and stones. Make sure there is space between the logs for frogs, toads and newts to move around. Then cover half of the top with soil and leaves but make sure you leave the entrance clear. You can then sprinkle wildflower seeds over the top or camouflage it with twigs and branches.

Don't fence us in!

Make a hole in your fence so wildlife can travel from one garden to the next. Animals like hedgehogs, frogs and toads need to be able to move across a large area to search for food and safe places to live.

Make a mini pond

You can make a small pond out of an old dish-washing bowl or container. First, build some stepping stones or a ramp so that wildlife can get in and out of your pond. Then add a layer of gravel in the bottom and fill it with water. Add a few water plants like pondweed and wait to see what arrives!

DID YOU FIND...

...the 15 hidden footprints from the beginning of the book?

16-17 Wonderful water

8-9 We are all unique

20-21 Happy birthday

10-11 Home sweet home

24-25 Finding nature

12-13 Everyone is talking

36-37 Sun seekers

40-41 We are all connected

42-43 Across the world

44-45 Planet of poop

46-47 Brilliant bones

48-49 Seriously smart

50-51 Super senses

52-53 Give and take

56-57 Give nature a helping hand

GLOSSARY

Learn to talk like a planet Earth expert

Migration

When animals or birds migrate, they travel to a different part of the planet at the same time each year. They travel to places with the best conditions for feeding, breeding and raising their young.

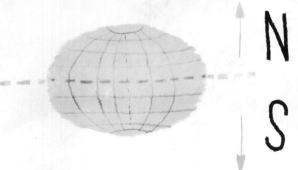

N
S

Hemisphere

A hemisphere is one half of the Earth. The Earth is divided into the Northern and Southern Hemisphere.

Species

A type of animal or plant. An endangered species is an animal or plant that is at risk of dying out and only a few are alive in the wild.

Ecosystem

A specific environment where plants, animals (including us humans) and living organisms all interact with each other and the landscape around them. Ecosystems can be as big as a rainforest or as small as a garden pond.

Global warming

The process that is causing the Earth's temperature to increase, leading to problems like forest fires and the ice caps melting.

Climate change

Changes in the Earth's weather over a long period of time caused by increased levels of gases like carbon dioxide.

INDEX

A

African wild dog 19
algae 39
ant 27, 49
Arctic tern 31
Australian mistletoe bird 45
autumn 28, 35

B

bactrian camel 17
bat 46
beetle 17, 44
blackbird 37
bones 6, 46–47
butterfly 15, 31, 55, 56

C

cactus 16
Canada geese 29
carbon dioxide 38–39
Caribbean reef squid 12
caribou 30

cat 36
cheetah 46
chipmunk 32
clam 20
coral 39
cow 44, 54
coyote 33
crab 6, 10
crocodile 7, 26

D

daisy 37
damselfly 40
desert 7, 16–17
dinosaur 21, 47
dolphin 48
dragonfly 22, 41
duck 23, 41

E

egg 7, 18, 22–23, 41
Egyptian plover 26
elephant 18

F

fallow deer 29
fava bean 13
feather 28–29
fish 6, 20, 27, 45
forest 24, 32, 44
fossil 21
frog 7, 23, 33, 41, 56
frogspawn 23
fur 28, 34

G

giant elephant ear plant 36
giraffe 9
goat 51
grass 24, 33
great horned owl 33

H

harvest mouse 10
hemisphere 42–43
horse 22, 44

K
kelp 39
kookaburra 55

L
leaves 28, 35
lion 19
lizard 7, 16, 37
lobster 6
lyrebird 12

M
mantis shrimp 51
moorhen 41
moth 51
mouse 32–33
mushroom 15, 35

N
nature 24
newt 7, 40, 56

O
ocean 39

octopus 48
orchid bee 26
oxygen 38–39

P
palm cockatoo 49
peregrine falcon 47
plastic 53
pond 6–7, 40–41, 57
poop 44–45

S
sand grouse 17
sea anemone 27
sea otter 54
seagrass 39
seaweed 39
skeleton 46
snail 14
snake 7, 28, 33, 47, 50
snowflake 9
soil 25
spider 6, 11
spring 34

squirrel 14, 48
summer 28, 32, 34–35, 42
sunshine 36–37

T
tadpole 40
tarsier 13
tiger cowrie 8
toad 40, 56–57
tree 7, 8, 20, 21, 27, 28,
       33, 38, 49

W
water 16–17
weaver bird 11
whale 6, 16, 31
white-fronted bee-eater 18
winter 28, 30, 34, 42

Z
zebra 8

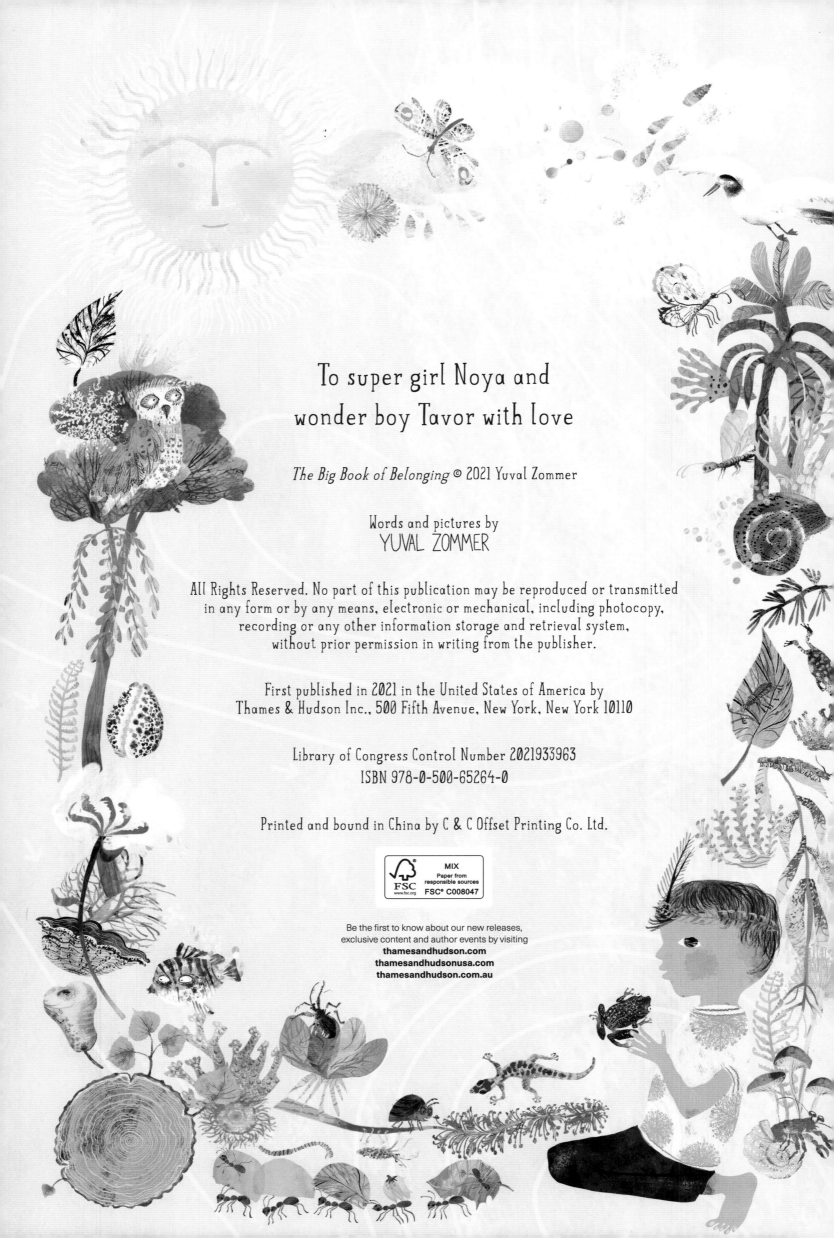

To super girl Noya and
wonder boy Tavor with love

The Big Book of Belonging © 2021 Yuval Zommer

Words and pictures by
YUVAL ZOMMER

First published in 2021 in the United States of America by
Thames & Hudson Inc., 500 Fifth Avenue, New York, New York 10110

Library of Congress Control Number 2021933963
ISBN 978-0-500-65264-0

Printed and bound in China by C & C Offset Printing Co. Ltd.